AF609211

SCIENCE OR BELIEF:
BRAIN WOULD IT BE THE SEAT OF OUR HEALING?

UNIVERSITY PICARDIE JULES VERNE
FACULTY OF MEDICINE OF AMIENS
UNIVERSITY SERVICE IN ALL LIFE LONG
SPACE FOR REFLECTION ETHICS REGIONAL OF PICARDIE

ACADEMIC YEAR 2016/2017

SCIENCE OR BELIEF: BRAIN WOULD IT BE THE SEAT OF OUR HEALING?

CRITIQUE OF MEDICAL HYPNOSIS AGAINST THE EXEGETICAL READING OF THE BIBLE

Presented by: M. Galien Ptolémée EKAZAMA

Strictly prohibited for sale

Translated from French by JSB Editions

ISBN 978-2-9561617-3-8

ACKNOWLEDGMENTS

To thank my Eternal Father...

... And to men who have contributed in this work:

- *professors*

- *Brother Yves for his lessons "Christians Interviews" online (www.entretienschretiens.com) - Copying authorization*

- *Brothers and Sisters of the Dokimos's association (www.lesdokimos.org)*

- *Brothers and Sisters of TV2vie team for uplifting education in conformity with the Word of God and for the BJC (Bible of Jesus Christ) (www.tv2vie.org)*

- *and other Brothers and Sisters in Christ for their involvement in the work of God ...*

- *... Beware lest anyone cheat you through philosophy and empty deceit, according to the tradition of men, according to the basic principles of the world, and not according to Christ.*

Colossians 2: 8

TABLE OF CONTENTS

INTRODUCTION

- *"Is hypnosis natural?"*
- *"Does the hypnotized person act like sleepwalker?"*
- *"What does it mean to be receptive or not to hypnosis?"*
- *"Will I be smarter with hypnosis?"*
- *"Does the hypnotist act like a magician?"*
- *"How does it feel when you are hypnotized?"*
- *"Do the hypnotized people play comedy?"*

Here are some questions that young children could ask about hypnotism.

It is true these questions may cause us to smile but depict an absolute reality. But, what is hypnosis exactly? And why is it used as an alternative therapy, the most integrated in the supply of care now?

We will also ask questions as medical doctors, seniors or juniors in our future practice of medicine. Wonder about the legitimacy of our exercise will depend on our ability to understand the patient as a whole but also to humiliate us, because of our powerlessness face of the limits of medicine.

"Then a dispute arose among them as to which of them would be greatest. And Jesus, perceiving the thought of their heart, took a little child and set him by Him, and said to them, "Whoever receives this little child in My name receives Me; and whoever receives Me receives Him who sent Me. For he who is least among you all will be great." [1]

---

1. Luke 9: 46-48

Do not forget that the Bible is a **historical** and **prophetic** book. The answers that we seek before asking the questions are indeed given by the Light of the Word of God. That is why we must take seriously these warnings:

"Knowing this first, that no prophecy of Scripture is of any private interpretation, for prophecy never came by the will of man, ***but holy men of God spoke as they were moved by the Holy Spirit."***[2]

From a historical perspective, it is necessary to remember that hypnosis has been used since ancient times and associated with magic and pagan religions (especially Egyptian). In ancient times, it has its corollary in a practice called "medicine by the dreams" in the rite of *incubation* with the antic Greek, associated with the cult of Asclepius (Aesculapius to the Roman, *his attribute is a pole around which wraps a serpent*[3], emblem of medicine these days). During incubation, the god intervened during sleep of the patient who was sleeping in the temple, to heal him and give him his orders.

This practice was formalized and covered with a "varnish" scientific by German medical doctor Franz Mesmer (1734-1815). He developed the theory of the animal magnetism, that the human body like the universe, is impregnated with an invisible magnetic fluid on which it was possible to act and whose disruption would cause diseases. Also, techniques to channel the fluid by "passes" on the body would activate the healing of the sick. Let's note that the power of the gaze also plays a major role in the transmission of said fluid.

Thereafter, the Marquis of Puységur (1751-1825), Mesmer's disciple undertook to continue the work and

2. 2 Peter 1: 20-21
3. See episode of the Bronze Serpent in the wilderness (Number 21: 4-9)

developed the *magnetic sleepwalking* state. He knew moreover a big hit with a young illiterate, foul-mouthed countryman, but who once in this state gave a totally supported speech and returned even medical diagnoses with which the correctness surprised the medical doctors. Despite these amazing results, this technique was not enough rational to be accepted by the Academy of Medicine.

The advance continued with James Braid (1795-1880), Scottish surgeon who denied the existence of a magnetic fluid but hypothesized a specific neurological condition: *the neuro hypnology* (referring to *Hypnos*, Greek god of sleep). He distinguished magnetism which was based previously as the power of the gaze and voice, by fixing the attention on a bright object, the aim is to cause eye fatigue.

Later, Jean-Martin Charcot, French neurologist (1825-1893) realized the work on hypnosis and hysteria. He recreates the hypnotic appearance and disappearance of symptoms. So he demonstrates that the hysteric paralyses are not determined by an organic lesion, but by the fact that he calls *a functional dynamic lesion*, and he considers that the hypnosis is a state appropriate to the hysteric people. At the same time, another current is developed by Hippolyte Bernheim (1840-1919), professor of the University of Nancy, which is opposed that of Charcot's point of view considering hypnosis as susceptible to therapeutic applications.

This is in the twentieth century, Milton Erickson (1901-1980), American psychiatrist laid the foundation of "ericksonian hypnosis" which considers "the trance is a common phenomenon, natural, that everyone knows in his ordinary life." It is on this premise that is based today, the practice of medical hypnosis as part of the management of pain, mobilizing patient's own resources to not perceive at least the time of the hypnotic trance neither pain nor anxiety...

Finally, from a biblical perspective, the Word of God is clear: *"**Give no regard to** mediums and familiar spirits; **do not seek after them**, to be defiled by them: I am the LORD your God"*[4]. The magnetic sleepwalking is not the work of God but of witchcraft, the human mind is manipulated under the influence of demons... Our spirit has been created to be exclusively in communion with the Spirit of God who has ability to heal all our diseases. Also, notice that the notion of spirit has no scientific connotation but rather religious even mystical!

The Bible tells us that *"knowledge puffs up, but love edifies"*[5]. Indeed, the advance of the science did not urge people to give glory to God, but rather to glory themselves inspired by pagan doctrines from antichrist origin.

You see, what connection is there between the God of the Bible and pagan gods in the historical context of hypnosis? Many who claim to be scientific in fact are still disciples of pagan gods, mystics, Freemasons or just great atheists...

"And what communion has light with darkness? And what accord has Christ with Belial [Satan]? "[6]

"Rather, that the things which the Gentiles [pagans] sacrifice they sacrifice to demons and not to God, and I do not want you to have fellowship with demons."[7]

*Therefore "**Come out from among them** and **be separate**, says the Lord. Do not touch what is unclean, and I will receive you."*[8]

4. Leviticus 19: 31
5. 1 Corinthians 8: 1
6. 2 Corinthians 6: 14-15
7. 1 Corinthians 10:20
8. 2 Corinthians 6:17

Christian as non-Christian moreover, should so shun the practice considered impure or unclean, according to the Word of God, whether in the fields of medicine (therapeutic hypnosis) or entertainment (magic shows).

We are going to see more clearly there, by confusing the doctrine of hypnosis to the healthy doctrine of the Word of God. Due to lack of information in the scientific literature about the clinical side effects of the practice of hypnosis, thus it seemed to us relevant to refocus this ancestral practice towards what Holy Scriptures brought to the humanity… then Science or Belief: brain would it be the seat of our healing?

So, in a thorough reading of the Bible (exegesis), we are going to wonder in the first place about safety of the practice of hypnosis (see the note by INSERM: National Institute of the Health and the Medical Research). Then we look for what makes the strength of a conviction in the healing process (belief or suggestion) to know the limits and dangers of the unconventional care practices (ethical and legal reflection).

I - BIBLE DISCUSSION: ABOUT SAFETY OF HYPNOSIS

The problem comes from the interpretation, the lack of understanding of phenomena beyond our intelligence. For it is not only a question of explaining that is to report causes, but especially to understand, that is manage to grasp the meaning, to reach the sense of conduct of other one accurately. The interpretation involves to try to put aside its own references and this even for a medical doctor or a therapist...

So, understanding that is not to judge. It is to recognize man in his experience, his unique story even if it seems strange, irrational or disproportionate compared to our standard, but important because gifted sense. Managing to grasp this sense therefore depends on our ability to listen, to access logic of the other even if foreign to our usual system. That is the discussion that opposes the practice of hypnosis (our usual system) to understanding of doctrine of the God of the Bible.

The opposition that exists between belief and knowledge is relative to a system of representation. Belief is an understanding constituted by information for which we hold to be true because based solely on trust (because no scientific element cannot prove it).

"Let no one deceive himself. If anyone among you seems to be wise in this age, let him become a fool that he may become wise. For ***the wisdom of this world is foolishness with God****. For it is written, "He catches the wise in their own craftiness"; and again, "The LORD knows the thoughts of the wise, that they are futile." Therefore let no one boast in men. For all things are yours"*[9].

The people who have the wisdom here, possess the knowledge, just like any information because non-integrated as an understanding representation system where God is at the centre (Christocentric).

"Can anyone teach God knowledge, since He judges those on high?"[10]

So that *"The heart of him who has understanding seeks knowledge, but the mouth of fools feeds on foolishness."*[11]

The place of God Jesus (means Yahweh is Salvation) is for the man who wants to walk with the true science by God and not by men, it should be a prime place in his decisions. It is in absolute confidence in God that the believer is called truly wise in God's eyes, see in the following Bible verses:

"Woe to the rebellious children, says the LORD, who take counsel, but not of Me, and who devise plans, ***but not of My Spirit, that they may add sin to sin****; who walk to go down to Egypt, and have not asked My advice, to strengthen themselves in the strength of Pharaoh, and to trust in the shadow of Egypt! Therefore the strength of Pharaoh shall be your shame, and trust in the shadow of Egypt shall be your humiliation."*[12]

"Woe to those who go down to Egypt for help, and rely on horses, who trust in chariots because they are many, and in horsemen because they are very strong, but who do not look to the Holy One of Israel, nor seek the LORD! Yet He also is wise and will bring disaster, and will not call back His words, but will arise against the house of evildoers, and against the help of those who work iniquity. ***Now the Egyptians are men, and not God; and their horses are flesh, and not spirit.*** *When the LORD stretches out His hand, both he who helps will fall,*

9. 1 Corinthians 3: 18-21
10. Job 21:22
11. Proverbs 15:14
12. Isaiah 30: 1-3

and he who is helped will fall down; they all will perish together."[13]

So, the best protection does not come from men nor from any human or even religious organization. While most men want protection from Pharaoh and support in the power of his chariots, that is to say a system of human organization; many fall into the sin of compromise. Thus, people who glory in men and believing to be wise are foolish because they seek truth in the world the approval of men rather than God. However, ***"The fear of the LORD is the beginning of knowledge**, but fools despise wisdom and instruction."*[14] .

And here are some instructions that Yahweh gives to His people before entering the Promised Land:

"When you come into the land which the LORD your God is giving you, ***you shall not learn to follow the abominations of those nations****. There shall not be found among you anyone who makes his son or his daughter pass through the fire, or one who practices witchcraft, or a soothsayer, or one who interprets omens, or a sorcerer, or one who conjures spells, or a medium, or a spiritist, or one who calls up the dead.* ***For all who do these things are an abomination to the LORD,*** *and because of these abominations the LORD your God drives them out from before you. You shall be blameless before the LORD your God. For these nations which you will dispossess listened to soothsayers and diviners; but as for you, the LORD your God has not appointed such for you."*[15]

The **abominations of Deuteronomy 18** in question, are numerous but not exhaustive, because some are still practised nowadays. Some of subtly disguised manner are used in the practice of medicine, particularly in unconventional care

13. Isaiah 31: 1-3
14. Proverbs 1: 7
15. Deuteronomy 18: 9-14

practices wide-ranging (acupuncture, mesotherapy, fire cutters, magnetism, relaxation therapy, transcendental meditation, hypnosis...). These are methods which did not make the proof of their harmlessness nor that of their efficiency. "**Adverse effects of unconventional care practices are poorly or not known, as there was no preliminary rigorous evaluation to their employment, and few or no published data. In addition, the professionals who use these unconventional care practices do not declare these adverse effects.**" reports the Ministry of the health (in France) in a statement updated on 06.13.2017[16]. As healthcare professionals, we have to understand these things how much important in the global care of the sick person (the sociocultural life, the spiritual life). The patient looks for personalized care which he does not find in the formal standardization of the conventional treatments which he considers unsuitable for his case. As medical doctor about us too, to be able to reach logic of the other one it is to question us as for the practice that we make of medicine.

Further to the analysis of these few passages of the Bible and the warnings given by the Ministry of the health, we want to put a highlight on the practice of hypnosis in medical environment. Since this practice is according to INSERM used as a complementary tool the most integrated into the offer of conventional care; it is relevant to ask the question of its safety and the occurrence of risk of adverse effects bound to this practice. Criticism is more on the doctrinal and the ethical aspect for lack of not being able to list the clinical adverse effects (because not known by medical profession this day).

However, God's Word says: ***"Thus says the LORD: Cursed is the man who trusts in man and makes flesh his strength, whose heart departs from the LORD."***[17]

16.http://social-sante.gouv.fr/soins-et-maladies/qualite-des-soins-et-pratiques/securite/article/pratiques-de-soins-non-conventionnelles
17. Jeremiah 17: 5

We understood that faith in God that is to testify our confidence in Him only, keeps us under His divine protection. Moreover, here is the promise that Yahweh makes for His people, for the one who chose the way of wisdom, to remain honourable with Yahweh and refuse to compromise in these abominations:

"If you diligently heed the voice of the LORD your God and do what is right in His sight, give ear to His commandments and keep all His statutes, ***I will put none of the diseases on you which I have brought on the Egyptians. For I am the LORD who heals you.****"*[18]

"Now see that I, even I, am He, and there is no God besides Me; I kill and I make alive; I wound and ***I heal****; nor is there any who can deliver from My hand."*[19]

The science of the healing only God holds it and He is still the only one to share it. He does not allow a third person to be deified, that a man is considered like Pharaoh swollen by human wisdom, and that he usurps the place of God in the believer's heart. Now this is what is made when the patient sets his heart in science of his doctor, in this particular case of hypnotherapist, yet without taking advice from Yahweh nor "to question His mouth." Here is what establishes an abomination in God's eyes: trust in men rather than God.

"For they loved the praise of men more than the praise of God."[20]

Now it is written: *"If any of you lacks wisdom,* ***let him ask of God, who gives to all liberally and without reproach, and it will be given to him****. But* ***let him ask in faith****, with no doubting, for he who doubts is like a wave of the sea driven*

18. Exodus 15:26
19. Deuteronomy 32:39
20. John 12: 43

and tossed by the wind. For let not that man suppose that he will receive anything from the Lord"[21] .

"As for these four young men, God gave them knowledge and skill in all literature and wisdom; and Daniel had understanding in all visions and dreams. (...) And in all matters of wisdom and understanding about which the king examined them, he found them ten times better than all the magicians and astrologers who were in all his realm."[22]

So we can easily understand that science according to God is not the same science according to men. Where God sees only madness and deceit, man sees wisdom and glory, but YAHWEH speaks: *"... who frustrates the signs of the babblers, and drives diviners mad; who turns wise men backward, and makes their knowledge foolishness"*[23].

"The wisdom of the prudent is to understand his way, but the folly of fools is deceit. Fools mock at sin, but among the upright there is favour. (...) ***There is a way that seems right to a man, but its end is the way of death."***[24]

Here is the main danger that constitutes science of Man, a science that is not just like God! "The man of science" according to God is foolish because he does not recognize his weakness, his limits, his guilt, he laughs at God and is not afraid of Him. His spirit is corrupted because it is not turned to God but rather turned to fables and God knows that their reasoning is futile because it does not bring healing but pulls rather death...

So apostle of Jesus Christ Paul warns us against those magicians, sorcerers, soothsayers, forecasters and hypnotists:

---

21. James 1: 5-7
22. Daniel 1: 17,20
23. Isaiah 44:25
24. Proverbs 14: 8-9.12

"Now I urge you, brethren, note those who cause divisions and offenses, contrary to the doctrine which you learned, and avoid them. For those who are such do not serve our Lord Jesus Christ, but their own belly, and ***by smooth words and flattering speech deceive the hearts of the simple****. For your obedience has become known to all. Therefore I am glad on your behalf; but I want you to be wise in what is good, and simple concerning evil."*[25]

Here "pure" has for Greek word "akeraios" also means "unmixed" (such some wine or metals), "spirit without mixture of the devil," "innocent", "simple". The warning concerns every believer who supports the healthy doctrine of the Word of God; they are called to separate from deceivers. Such people are the ones who commit the abominations of Deuteronomy 18: 9-14. Hypnosis is part of it, in spite of the list is not exhaustive... according to the Bible hypnotist is similar to magician, deceiver, false doctor, forecaster (used to decipher and interpret a dream that the king had, see Daniel 1: 17, 20). Hypnotism is not a science that comes from God, and Apostle Paul warns his disciple Timothy:

"O Timothy! Guard what was committed to your trust, ***avoiding the profane and idle babblings and contradictions of what is falsely called knowledge*** *— by professing it some have strayed concerning the faith."*[26]

"Now the Spirit expressly says that in latter times some will depart from the faith, giving heed to ***deceiving spirits*** *and* ***doctrines of demons****, speaking lies in hypocrisy, having their own conscience seared with a hot iron "*[27].

25. Romans 16: 17-19
26. 1 Timothy 6: 20-21
27. 1 Timothy 4: 1-2

The expression "seared with a hot iron" or "mark of the flail" is *"kauteriazo"* in Greek and means "those whose soul is stigmatized by the marks of sin." In a medical sense, it means "cauterizing". This passage refers to the mark of the Beast (Satan) that will be printed in the consciousness of men; that is why God asks real believers to keep His Word in their hearts (Psalm 119: 11). However, hypnosis also affects the consciousness and thoughts of people who fall into the hypnotic trance ...Our actions are the results of our thoughts; we think and we act. Yet if we believe the Word of God, we act according to it. Those who have mark of the Beast, they think and act as it. They are as manipulated, losing their own will because controlled; following the example of hypnotist who prints a mark in the minds of those who listen to him. They will believe that thoughts running through their minds come from themselves but in truth they will be inspired by deceiving spirits and doctrines of demons!

These people are not with God because they have turned their heart to doctrines of demons rather than simplicity of the healthy doctrine, which is the Word of God; they corrupted in sin and thus they lost the protection of the hand of God. That is why Paul adds to those who remained honourable up to the end with God: *"For our boasting is this: the testimony of our conscience that we conducted ourselves in the world* ***in simplicity and godly sincerity****, not with fleshly wisdom but by the grace of God."*[28]

"But I fear, lest somehow, as the serpent deceived Eve by his craftiness, ***so your minds may be corrupted from the simplicity that is in Christ.****"*[29]

Consciousness and thoughts corrupted because they did not want to obey the voice of God, His word, they did not listen to His commands and therefore did not know real

---

28. 2 Corinthians 1:12
29. 2 Corinthians 11: 3

healing. *"For the hearts of this people have grown dull. Their ears are hard of hearing, and their eyes they have closed, lest they should see with their eyes and hear with their ears, lest they should understand with their hearts and turn,* ***so that I should heal them****"*[30].

"For the time will come when they will not endure sound doctrine, but according to their own desires, because they have itching ears, ***they will heap up for themselves teachers; and they will turn their ears away from the truth, and be turned aside to fables.****"*[31]

The doctors here are the ones who possess authority to teach and human knowledge (read: fleshly wisdom). In several places the Bible teaches us to move away from such people who are hypocrites, deceivers, swollen by fleshly wisdom, corrupted by doctrines of demons, false doctors, foolish because they did not listen to the Word of God but rather their bellies... But now men preferred to find refuge with other men, magicians, forecasters and hypnotists who abandoned God and His simplicity in His healing promise made for men.

Men turned away from The Truth and rather turned to fables, seduced by "gentle words and flatteries" and by "pleasant speech"! So the practice of hypnosis is it a fable? Isn't it without danger? We questioned safety of hypnosis about a doctrinal point of view in the exegetical reading of certain passages of the Bible. In the second part, we shall try to understand how involve faith and suggestion in the healing process...

---

30. Matthew 13:15
31. 2 Timothy 4: 3-4

II – FROM THE POWER OF BELIEF TO SELF-SUGGESTION IN THE PATIENT

II.1 WOULD THE PRAYER HAVE A HEALING EFFICIENCY?

"Then they journeyed from Mount Hor by the Way of the Red Sea, to go around the land of Edom; and the soul of the people became very discouraged on the way. And the people spoke against God and against Moses: "Why have you brought us up out of Egypt to die in the wilderness? For there is no food and no water, and our soul loathes this worthless bread." So the LORD sent fiery serpents among the people, and they bit the people; and many of the people of Israel died. Therefore the people came to Moses, and said, "We have sinned, for we have spoken against the LORD and against you; pray to the LORD that He take away the serpents from us." So Moses prayed for the people. ***Then the LORD said to Moses, "Make a fiery serpent, and set it on a pole; and it shall be that everyone who is bitten, when he looks at it, shall live."*** *So Moses made a bronze serpent, and put it on a pole; and so it was, if a serpent had bitten anyone, when he looked at the bronze serpent, he lived."*[32]

This episode of the exodus of Hebrew in the desert of Sinai illustrates the power that God has on people. This attitude that people complain against God and blame Him for what happened to them established a grave sin against God. People have sinned by speaking against the LORD. It is when God's

32. Numbers 21: 4-9

judgment was going to beat on the nation. These fiery serpents are actually venomous serpents (hence the burning sensation caused by their bites). Thus people were perishing in the desert just like the world is perishing because of the poison of sin. In fact, man is dying spiritually because sin prevents him from having access to real source of life: GOD!

Only God can give life to this world that is perishing poisoned by sin.

"...nor let us tempt Christ, as some of them also tempted, and were destroyed by serpents; nor complain, as some of them also complained, and were destroyed by the destroyer. Now all these things happened to them as examples, and they were written for our admonition, upon whom the ends of the ages have come."[33]

The first verb "tempt" from Greek "ekpeirazo" means test; experience the character of God and his power. The second "tempt" from Greek "peirazo" means try if something can be done; experience mischievously, cleverly, to prove his feelings and his judgments; try or test faith, virtue, character by seduction of sin; to seek to sin; to inflict pain in order to experience. This term is also used when men want to tempt God by showing their distrust, by a wicked or evil conduct, to experience justice and patience of God, and to challenge Him, to urge Him to give proof of His perfections. Here is how people sinned against God by attempting Him in the wilderness...

"And as ***Moses lifted up the serpent in the wilderness, even so must the Son of Man be lifted up****, that whoever believes in Him should not perish but have eternal life."*[34] These verses echo that of the book of Numbers 21 verse 9: *"So Moses made a bronze serpent, and put it on a pole; and so it was, if a serpent had bitten anyone, when he looked at the bronze serpent, he lived".*

33. 1Corinthians 10: 9-11
34. John 3: 14-15

God in His grace gives antidote against poison that is sin. This pole is the banner which corresponds to the instruction or order that God gives to people to heal them. God brings up on a pole, on the cross, His Son Jesus. And the Word of God tells us that if we look at this cross, we shall be saved. The Bronze serpent rolled up on the pole prefigured the death of Lord Jesus...

Bronze speaks to us about the judgment (Job 20:24) and speaks of fire that melts metal to make the Bronze serpent. This metal constituted tools used in sign of purity and incorruptibility during the sacrifices of animals made on the altar of atonement by the priests chosen by God:

"Then the LORD spoke to Moses, saying: "Tell Eleazar, the son of Aaron the priest, to pick up the censers out of the blaze, for they are holy, and scatter the fire some distance away. The censers of these men who sinned against their own souls, let them be made into hammered plates as a covering for the altar. Because they presented them before the LORD, therefore they are holy; and they shall be a sign to the children of Israel." So Eleazar the priest took the bronze censers, which those who were burned up had presented, and they were hammered out as a covering on the altar"[35].

The Bronze serpent also speaks to us about the curse of Genesis 3: 14, Serpent must be put in the fire during the judgment of God; so that Jesus can save us also from our sins, He also had to undergo the cutting heat of the fire that will lead Him then to the end by the death on the cross. So pole talks about the cross, Jesus is represented here by a serpent made in bronze; Paul tells us in 2 Corinthians 5:21 *"For He made Him* [Jesus] *who knew no sin to be sin for us, that we might become the righteousness of God in Him."*

35. Numbers 16: 36-39

Moreover, words **"lift up"** as Moses lifted up pole to the Bronze serpent in the wilderness, thus referred to Christ lifted up on the cross that is executed on the cross, crucified. So Jesus has borne our curses, sins and diseases on the cross. Here is all the wisdom and the power of God are madness to men!

*"He is despised and rejected by men, a Man of sorrows and acquainted with grief. And we hid, as it were, our faces from Him; He was despised, and we did not esteem Him. Surely **He has borne our griefs and carried our sorrows**; yet we esteemed Him stricken, smitten by God, and afflicted. But He was wounded for our transgressions, He was bruised for our iniquities; the chastisement for our peace was upon Him, **and by His stripes we are healed**."*[36]

For what purpose must the Son of Man be lifted up? John 3:15 *"... that whoever **believes in Him** should not perish but have eternal life."* The Son of Man must be lifted up by the ground so that man can have access to eternal life, so that humanity can be saved. But the salvation or the deliverance will only be the privilege of those who believe in the work of the cross; so healing is only accessible for person who **believes in God**.

But what to believe? What does that imply from us? How people were saved in Numbers 21? By looking at the Bronze serpent. How can we be saved in John 3? By believing in God, to Lord Jesus. Faith is described by the words "to look at" in Numbers 21 while we have its equivalent in the word "to believe" in John 3. In other words, faith which saved people in Numbers 21, is faith which motivated them to follow God's instruction to look at the Bronze serpent. Similarly, faith which saves in John 3 is faith which motivates you to believe in Jesus Christ and to trust in His word. We could paraphrase John 3: 14-15 as follows: "Just like the fact of looking at the serpent

36. Isaiah 53: 3-5

that Moses raised in the desert saved people dying of poison, anyone who believes in the Son of man and trusts His words also have eternal life." The Hebrew word for “look” refers to a very attentive look by the sick person on the Bronze serpent. In the book of Hebrew 12: 2, *"looking unto Jesus, the author and finisher of our faith",* we understand easily that is not a question at all of having a simple look to Jesus... Faith which heals and which saves is an unwavering, deep faith in Jesus who appeals to all our person, our heart, our soul, our will and our thoughts.

Re-reading this story of snakes in the book of Numbers, it is justifiable at first sight to be sceptic, to ask the following questions: How does look something can save a person? How can a snake-metal made save a person who is dying by a poisoned bite? The answer is very simple. After analysis, it is not the Bronze serpent that saves. It is God who saves. This piece of metal itself has no healing properties. It would be foolish to believe in that! In truth, we are saved by God's power through prayer that are addressed to Him with faith (as Moses prayed for the people who spoke to Yahweh). Similarly, when you look at Jesus hanging on the cross, it is not His body that heals us from our sins. Lord Jesus says it Himself: *"It is the Spirit who gives life; the flesh profits nothing. The words that I speak to you are spirit, and they are life"* in John 6:63. It is by faith in the word of Jesus that we are saved. In other words, it is when we decide to trust in God by submitting our life in act of obedience to the instructions of the Bible that God's power can act in us **to save** us from the power of sin and **to heal** us.

NB "Sozo" in Greek, means both to save and to heal, used in Scripture it refers to the "salvation" by the forgiveness of the sins.

II.2 DISCERNMENT FROM THE TRUTH ... TO THE PLACEBO

But what is faith really? ***"Now faith is the substance of things hoped for, the evidence of things not seen."***[37] Let us take a striking example in the Gospel where faith was manifested through man struck of blindness for many years.

"Now they came to Jericho. As He went out of Jericho with His disciples and a great multitude, blind Bartimaeus, the son of Timaeus, sat by the road begging. And when he heard that it was Jesus of Nazareth, he began to cry out and say, "Jesus, Son of David, have mercy on me!" Then many warned him to be quiet; but he cried out all the more, "Son of David, have mercy on me!" So Jesus stood still and commanded him to be called. Then they called the blind man, saying to him, "Be of good cheer. Rise, He is calling you." And throwing aside his garment, he rose and came to Jesus. So Jesus answered and said to him, "What do you want Me to do for you?" The blind man said to Him, "Rabboni, that I may receive my sight" ***Then Jesus said to him, "Go your way; your faith has made you well." And immediately he received his sight and followed Jesus on the road."***[38]

Believe without seeing! Here is the demonstration of the faith of Bartimaeus who made present things for he hoped as proof of his faith. The story of Bartimaeus shows man whose faith held attention of Jesus. Although a blinded-man physical he had a good spiritual sight. He did not see but he could hear people that spoke, *"So then faith comes by hearing, and hearing by the word of God."*[39] This man has recognized God well. We read that he "followed Jesus on the road" verse 52, and glorified God in recognition of his healing as Luke 18: 43 added. His faith in Jesus Christ allowed him to see again. It

37. Hebrew 11: 1
38. Mark 10: 46-52
39. Romans 10: 17

does not mean that faith is the cause of recovering of sight. It means that faith of Bartimaeus opened source of infinite grace that caused healing. Faith in itself has no magic virtue. It only allows God's power to effect healing. It is comparable to valve which opens and allows to pass flow of divine power... So it is not a question of seeing with fleshly eyes because it was useless for the blind man to recognize Jesus as Messiah promised by God to save men. So, this discernment is took place on a spiritual level where Bartimaeus wholeheartedly convince the divinity of Jesus_ Yahweh is Salvation; *"For we walk by faith, not by sight"*[40]. Lord Jesus wants to make us understand here that God's power is accessible to those who by faith open Him their heart. Conversely, all that power is not available to person who, by his incredulity closed the door in grace offered by God. So that is what tells us prophet Isaiah in the Old Testament:

"Keep on hearing, but do not understand; ***keep on seeing, but do not perceive."***[41]

"And in them the prophecy of Isaiah is fulfilled, which says: 'Hearing you will hear and shall not understand, and ***seeing you will see and not perceive****; for the hearts of this people have grown dull. Their ears are hard of hearing, and* ***their eyes they have closed, lest they should see with their eyes*** *and hear with their ears, lest they should understand with their hearts and turn,* ***so that I should heal them****."*[42]

It does not necessarily just have to be blind not to see and not to discern what is true or false: from the truth... to the placebo! It is necessary to be especially struck by a spiritual blindness which dives into darkness that keep in blindness of spiritual eyes because of state of the heart. The heart plays the role of receptacle for God'word because we do not listen with

40. 2 Corinthians 5: 7
41. Isaiah 6: 9
42. Matthew 13: 14-15

our ears, we do not see with our fleshly eyes, but we understand with our heart the word of God.

Also *"**The lamp of the body is the eye.** If therefore your eye is good, your whole body will be full of light. But if your eye is bad, your whole body will be full of darkness. If therefore the light that is in you is darkness, how great is that darkness!"*[43]

Here, we understand eye like a spiritual perception. We make regularly this kind of link for vision when we do not appeal to eye of the body but to eye of the mind. For example, when we ask: "Do you see what I mean?" The interest of the question is not to know if it is possible to see with eyes what is verbally said! By this question, we can understand: "Does your intelligence, the eye of your mind manage to capture what I want to say?" In this case, we see with our intellectual faculty. Our mind is like an eye that allows us to see in the sense of understanding ideas. In the same way, we also have "spiritual eyes" with which we perceive spiritual truths. Then it becomes possible to discern glory of God (such as Bartimaeus that discerned it though he is a blind person).

Very often, people fail to grasp significance of message of the Gospel because they have a lack of spiritual perception (not because they are lacking intelligence). The Bible describes this gap by comparing it with blindness. The spiritual blindness prevents human beings from understanding truths of the spiritual world. Gold, *"**The spirit of a man is the lamp** of the LORD, searching all the inner depths of his heart."*[44] We can easily make link between spirit and eye. The parallel is established as follows: eye is in the human body what spirit of the man is in his soul. Just like our eyes of flesh perceive the physical environment, our spirit can distinguish truths of the spiritual world; hence importance of having a good spiritual sight!

---

43. Matthew 6: 22-23
44. Proverbs 20: 27

When Jesus speaks about a "good eye" in Matthew 6:22, on a physical level, it also refers to eye that converges light in the right place that is in a single meeting point. There is no two or several points of convergence. There is only one. In this case eye in good condition is an eye which is "single" or “simple”, an eye which converges light to a single focus. It is also translation that gives us Darby Bible[45] : *"The lamp of the body is the eye; if therefore thine* ***eye be single****, thy whole body shall be full of light",* it means that our ability to see spiritually is directly connected with vision which must be simple; relating to a dedicated unit, to concentration of attention, or still to an undivided heart. Let us note parallelism between words "heart" and "eye" that are exchangeable terms in some biblical passages. For instance, Psalm 119: 10, 15:

"With my whole heart I have sought You; Oh, let me not wander from Your commandments!"

"I will meditate on Your precepts, and contemplate Your ways."

So a simple eye or a whole heart are words that evoke the same unity of intention, that to converge all our attention and our energy on God and only God. One thing is simple if it is not subject of division. For example, if our eyes sometimes look here and sometimes look over there without any coordination; our vision will be affected. The opposite of a simple vision is a double vision, in a medical term we speak about *diplopia*; Jesus speaks about a "badly-disposed eye." This same disorder can also occur with our spiritual perception. Instead of paying all our attention on God, we have one eye fixed to God and an other one fixed to another source of interest. Then we speak about a problem of spiritual diplopia.

45. This translation of the Bible speaks of a "single eye" that is to say, in good condition or healthy eye in other versions.

In the case of influence under hypnosis, this other source of interest is the human mediator on whom all our attention converges. We read in Luke 11:35, warning that echoes passage from Matthew 6:22: *"The lamp of the body is the eye. Therefore, when your eye is good, your whole body also is full of light. But when your eye is bad, your body also is full of darkness.* ***Therefore take heed that the light which is in you is not darkness."*** In other words, "Make sure that you have light in you and not darkness." What Lord Jesus is telling us here, it is that each person believes that he perceives correctly and he has enough light to see. Each man believes that his vision of things, his beliefs, his perception of life correspond to the truth. Yet it is not there because: "You think you see, but in truth you are in darkness." It is only the placebo effect that persuades healing, but in truth it is state of blindness... So, isn’t that the sort of thing we talk about in blind test during clinical trials? Even double-blind test when neither the medical doctor nor the patient know nature of studied drugs??

II.3 THE PRACTICE HYPNOSIS IN THE HOSPITAL

The placebo effect is the impact of medication or act, not attributable to the intrinsic property of the administered drug, since devoid of active ingredient. The placebo effect belongs rather to a relationship between therapist and his patient. Thus the suggestion has an important place in the implementation of the placebo effect. That is why hypnosis is considered as a form of the placebo effect but is not just in it as we have already understood. Besides, hypnosedation was developed by Marie-Elisabeth Faymonville professor in the University Hospital of Liege (Belgium) in 1992. Hypnosedation aims to amplify resources of anxiolytique and analgesia in the patients. It combines hypnosis and intravenous conscious sedation and is used today as alternative to general anaesthesia. The team of Pr. Faymonville was interested in the modulating role of hypnosis in pain through the functional imaging by PET scan (Positron Emission Tomography).

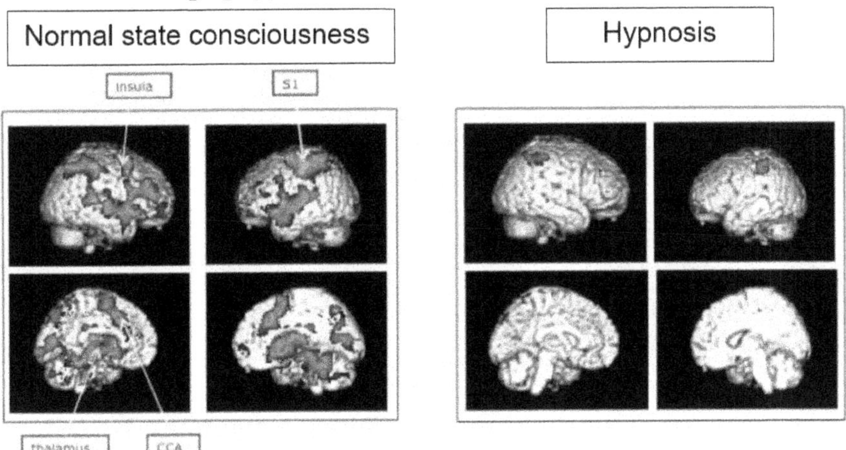

Representation of the activated cerebral areas during a painful stimulation in the normal state of consciousness (left panel) or hypnosis (right panel). In normal consciousness, the anterior cingulate cortex (CCA) and the neural network involved in pain (Pre-frontal cortex, pre-supplementary motor area (S1) striatum, insular and per-genual cortices, thalami and brainstem) are activated. In a hypnotic state, activation of these regions by pain stimuli is attenuated.

(Illustrations from work by Hick G., Faymonville ME. Hypnosis in anaesthesia. 53° Congress of the French Society of Anaesthesia Resuscitation. 2011)

It is in this therapeutic framework that self-suggestion inscribed; where the anaesthesiologist in the operating block helps patients to use their own resources to not perceive any more, at least the time of the operation, their pain and / or anxiety. However, here is in another frame, that of the Creation in Book of Genesis 2:21, the first surgical operation of thoracotomy with the "spiritual sedation" done when *"the LORD God caused a deep sleep to fall on Adam, and he slept; and He took one of his ribs, and closed up the flesh in its place."*

III - WHERE IS THE DANGER?

III.1 WHAT DOES THE LAW SAY?

What follows are data extracted from report meta-analysis of INSERM, in June 2015: Evaluation of effectiveness of the practice of hypnosis, pp.12-13, 16, and 136.

"In France, **there is no specific legal** framework governing the practice of hypnosis. **The UD [University Diploma] of hypnosis are not recognized by the College of medical doctors.** According to the regulations, the medical doctor is not thus allowed to mention these practices on his plate and/or his orders. On his side, the health insurance does not support hypnosis sessions. There is a code act in the common classification of medical acts labelled "hypnosis session for analgesic" (ANRP001 code), but this act is not refundable (rate fixed to 0 euros). If hypnotherapy is practised by a panel doctor within framework of his consultation, the consultation remains supported by the health insurance (according to the usual rules of refund)."

"... Other organizations propose trainings for all, not reserved for only healthcare professionals, which lifts ethical questions (see note on safety). These organizations do not adhere to code of ethics of the Francophone Confederation of Hypnosis and Brief Therapies (CFHTB) and very often **do not have their own code of ethics.** In addition, some of their trainings are certified "therapeutic hypnosis," and it is necessary to call back that if there is no legal text prohibiting exemption of these trainings to not healthcare professionals, **the practice of hypnosis to the therapeutic purposes by non-doctors has already object of condemnations[46] for illegal**

practice of medicine (Article L.4161-1 of the Code of Public Health [in France])."

But according to this report by INSERM: [National Institute of Health And Medical Research], hypnosis is one of the most integrated unconventional practices to conventional care offering. "The use of alternative therapies in the developed countries is growing, with a particular development observed in area of the supportive care including oncology. That can partly be explained by the fact that unconventional practices take into account needing to focus on quality of life when healing is not possible (Roberti di Sarsina 2007). "

[...]

"**Rather, challenge seems to be at the ethical and legal level.** Already, the practice of hypnosis is framed by ethical charters, **but to date, there is no clear legal framework** to better define the risk..."

46. Court of Appeal, Toulouse, Chamber of Criminal Appeals 3, on 17 February 2009 - No. 08/00429, 203/09 and No. 09-81.778 of the Criminal Chamber on 09 March 2010

III.2 LOSS OF CONTROL OF THE BODY, THE SOUL AND THE SPIRIT

The side effects that seem to be inherent to hypnosis are situated at first on a doctrinal point of view; then on absence of the strict legal framework. More generally, the question of the **ethical-legal risk** and risks of psychological manipulations (e.g., induction of false memories of sexual abuses in the childhood) testify of a loss of control on the part of some practitioners of hypnosis and always a loss of will control those who listen to them! A report of an University degree in medical hypnosis (Keke 2014) having been interested on the subject of ethical-legal risk in hypnosis, identified 16 judicial decisions involving hypnosis, including 15 concerning of the facts took place in France. Those were mostly cases of rapes or sexual assaults of patients put into the hypnotic trance by their practitioner or a third person, case of the illegal practice of medicine, or the use of hypnosis during procedures of justice. **Six cases of sexual assaults incriminate one doctor in two cases**, one osteopath in one case, one "magnetizer" in one case, one "hypnotist" non-doctor in one case, and a third person (friend / family) in the last case .

Let us still specify risk induced by the loss of control of the body, the soul and the spirit within framework of the practice of hypnosis. Technique called dissociation in the therapeutic hypnosis is to disable the critical consciousness of the subject, usually either by focusing attention on a specific item, either by creating some confusion. This is a fundamental technique of hypnotism: be there and somewhere else, like the one who is suffering from a spiritual perception disorder (see II.2 "spiritual diplopia").

But then what spirit is? From the healthy doctrine of God spirit is the breath of life, indeed *"and the LORD God formed man of the dust of the ground, and breathed into his nostrils the breath of life; and man became a living being."*[47]

So that spirit is not belong to God, that is who does not focus his attention towards God (following the example of the Bronze serpent); this spirit lost every control because it is suffering from double vision even of a spiritual blindness, the Bible speaks about an extinct spirit.

*"Now may the God of peace Himself sanctify you completely; and may your whole **spirit**, **soul**, and **body** be preserved blameless at the coming of our Lord Jesus Christ."*[48]

We have already included in several verses importance to stay honourable to God, to fix his look, his attention towards God, to keep a whole heart to Him and Him alone.

*"That each of you should know how to possess his own **vessel*** [read: his own body] *in sanctification and honour, not in passion of lust, like the Gentiles* [pagans] *who do not know God"*[49].

The personal sanctification is for every believer who knows God and who has to supply an effort by using daily the Word of God and prayer, to keep in sanctification. Do not comply with his lusts implies separation from sin and bad companies according to 2 Corinthians 6: 14-18. The believers in God who stay in sanctification carry necessarily the fruits of the Spirit of God: *"But the fruit of the Spirit is love, joy, peace, longsuffering, kindness, goodness, faithfulness, [23] gentleness, **self-control**."*[50] Yet loss of control of body in the practice of

47. Genesis 2: 7
48. 1 Thessalonians 5:23
49. 1 Thessalonians 4: 4-5
50. Galatians 5:22-23

hypnosis pulls immediately loss of self-control and besides loss of control of spirit!

"Or do you not know that ***your body is the temple of the Holy Spirit*** *who is in you, whom you have from God, and you are not your own? For you were bought at a price; therefore glorify God* ***in your body and in your spirit, which are God's****."*[51]

To understand better interaction between the spirit, the soul and the body, we drawn up three figures:

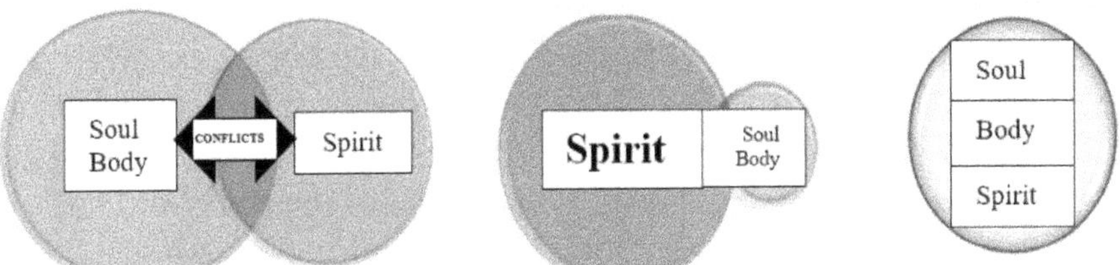

Fig. 1: **Child in the faith** *Fig. 2* **Acquisition of the maturity** *Fig. 3 :* **Man accomplished Spiritual harmony with God**

(Figures taken from http://chretiens2000.over-blog.com/2016/11/mon-ame-discipline-toi.html)

Transformation allows child in faith to grow spiritually. Indeed, every child of God is called to become mature, to move from infant to that young man, until that the father according to 1 John 2: 12-14.*"For everyone who partakes only of milk is unskilled in the* ***word of righteousness****, for he is a babe. But solid food belongs to those who are of full age, that is, those who by reason of* ***use*** *have their senses* ***exercised*** *to discern both good and evil."*[52] The word "babe" in this passage comes from Greek "nepios" means "ignoramus".

51. 1 Corinthians 6: 19-20
52. Hebrews 5: 13-14, New King James Version highlights from the bold words difficulty of work of the Christian "full-aged" or "completed"

Transformation involves change "to be born again" to his whole being (spirit, soul, body) is either completely subjected to his own will but God's. As soon as the one who shelters in his body the temple of the Holy Spirit; his body belongs to God and the Holy Spirit communicates directly with human spirit. Lusts and the evil influences are then chased away towards rest of the being which is the soul and the body. This little voice inside that guides us to do well, so this is the Holy Spirit who teaches it to our spirit of man, according to John 14:26. Whereas soul which is attached to the physical body seeks to satisfy desires of the fleshly lusts (**Fig. 1:** conflicts into "child in the faith"). The believer is urged not to comply his own lusts but to oust sins that so come from his soul (the flesh). He must show the fruits of the Spirit of God to silence the voice of the soul and submit it completely forward to God's will (**Fig. 2:** Acquisition of the maturity). This is not automatic, it takes time (**experiment**), efforts (**exercises**), some experiment (**use**) in everyday life! So the believer finishes making that the Word of God asks, worth knowing "to be completely" (spirit, soul, body) to God (**Fig. 3**: Man accomplished). In the light of this analysis, we understand that it is on the spirit of man that God acts to heal him.

But hypnosis also acts on the spirit of man; we understand now the consequences (false memories, rapes, etc.); loss of control of spirit and body induced by hypnotherapist who actually usurps God's place in the spirits of people... But what the Word of God's answers:

*"Now **the Spirit** expressly says that in latter times some will depart from the faith, giving heed to **deceiving spirits and doctrines of demons**"*[53]

"For they loved the praise of men more than the praise of God."[54]

53. 1 Timothy 4: 1
54. John 12: 43

"And for this reason God will send them ***strong delusion****, that they should believe the lie, that they all may be condemned who did not believe the truth but had pleasure in unrighteousness."*[55]

The Bible declares to us that the real usurper is not man as hypnotist, but the spirit of delusion associated with it, sent by God to adhere them even more in their lies; men will believe in doctrines of demons just like glory of the men rather than God's. Satan is this spirit of delusion, deceiver, liar, it persuades lie in some people that healing will be obtained with men, in this case by hypnotherapists... So Satan usurps God's place in mind of people! So they will keep believing that thoughts running through their minds come from themselves but in truth, they will be inspired by devils...

In conclusion, doctrine of **hypnotism is non-conformity** with the healthy doctrine of the Word of God. The side effects about that we discussed in the beginning of this chapter are linked. From a doctrinal point of view, at first that the practice of hypnosis is a gateway to spirits of demons, so not glorifying God but Man. Then, from a legal point of view, the ethical-legal risk appears to be increased because of ambiguity that hangs around this practice in medicine; the diploma of which is not yet recognized by the College of medical doctors in France!

---

55. 2 Thessalonians 2: 11-12, New King James Version says "strong delusion" when other versions speak of "spirit".

III.3 CALL FOR VIGILANCE AND SOBRIETY

The evidence-based medicine seems to get out of breath and to be increasingly shunned by the patients who are looking for a more human and personalized medicine. Hypnosis is presented as additional therapy increasingly used in the hospital; this practice gives impression of the patient to be a care actor.

"The use of such practices would be based more on the quest of a coherence with his own values, beliefs and philosophies of life and health than on a disappointing experience of the conventional medicine (Astin on 1998). Prevention and desire for a healthy lifestyle are other motives for appeal. Moreover, the part of self-health management has increased in recent years, and the subjects readily turn to unconventional practices, **by considering that what is natural is without danger** (which is not necessarily true, WHO [World Health Organization] 2013). "[56]

For example, **shamanism** is not without danger...?

Shaman is considered like a <u>sorcerer</u>, <u>diviner</u>, <u>healer</u> with **occult power**, enters into a **hypnotic trance** caused by drug use that would allow him to blind his spirit with the world of the invisible and "to unite with the gods" or the spirits of devils. The word "witchcraft" is used on the Bible for *"mageia"* in Greek (which means in English: magic) or *"pharmakeia"* in Greek (gives pharmacy or drugs). Shaman takes drugs to reach a **state of consciousness modified** so as to contact unclean "spirits" that would confer on him knowledge and "magic powers". In a general way, the **"setting hypnotic trance"** can be obtained by kinaesthetic processes (dance, chorea), by sound rhythmical and repetitive (song), by adding it change of the physical appearance (suit, mask, make-up). **Drunkenness**

---

56. INSERM report, in June 2015: Evaluation of effectiveness of the practice of hypnosis, p.12

is also looked for in alcoholic drinks placing shaman as intermediary between people and the gods...

Now The God of the Bible never stops warning us concerning these false prophets:

*"If a man should walk in a false spirit and speak a lie, saying, '**I will prophesy to you of wine and drink**' even he would be the prattler* [prophet] *of this people."*[57]

But the believers who have received the Holy Spirit manifest gifts of the Spirit of God discerning by the spiritual eyes darkness from light.

*"You are all sons of light and sons of the day. We are not of the night nor of darkness. **Therefore let us not sleep**, as others do, but **let us watch and be sober**. For those who sleep, sleep at night, and **those who get drunk are drunk at night**."*[58]

As this is a call to watch and to stay sober as for the proliferation of unconventional care practices that keep growing out of biblical context...

57. Micah 2: 11
58. 1 Thessalonians 5: 5-7

CONCLUSION

After this exegetical study of Bible verses, we were seized by the correctness of criticism around the practice of hypnosis. That says no verse of the Bible specifically mentions the term "hypnosis". But, according to the origins, hypnosis comes from Greek *hypno* "sleep." According to the medical Larousse Dictionary, hypnosis is *"technique capable of inducing partial sleep state, different from the usual sleep."* In fact, we must understand that the hypnotic trance fall us into a sleep... spiritually!

So all the studied verses "agree" to say that this practice is against the will of God; through His Word, the God of the Bible, Jesus who also means Yahweh is Salvation condemns hypnotism and its consequences. The adverse effects arising directly or indirectly around this practice are the object of many current medical researches. Nevertheless, this is on the doctrinal and ethical-legal point of view that the issue of safety of hypnosis rather seems to settle.

Besides, increasingly unconventional care practices earn the western medicine based on evidences (EBM: Evidence Based Medicine). So how this medicine will face the development of unconventional practices against the offense of illegal practice of medicine? And how will it have to answer phenomena that affect the spiritual domain?

ABSTRACT

We have stayed true to the Scriptures, "glued" as close as possible to sacred texts without adding or subtracting. The following Bible verses summarize in a few lines the objective sought at this critical analytical work of the practice of hypnosis in medicine and call to alert the public health: *"And do not participate in the unfruitful works of darkness, but otherwise expose them! For it is shameful to say the things they do in secret; but all that is condemned is manifest by the light, because the light is that which manifests everything. This is why it is said, Awake, O sleeper, and arise from the dead, and Christ will shine on you. Take care to drive you carefully, not as fools, but as wise, redeeming the time, because the days are evil. Therefore do not be foolish, but understand what the will of the Lord. And be not drunk with wine in which there is dissolution, but be filled with the Spirit".* (Ephesians 5: 11-18, New King James Version)

Keywords: hypnosis; Bible; healing; alternative medicine.

BIBLIOGRAPHY

- Bible of Darby
- Bible of Jesus Christ (BJC), 2015-2016 Edition. Available on :https://www.bibledejesuschrist.org/lire.html
- Bible of Louis Segond 1910
- New King James Version (NKJV) (most quoted unless otherwise stated)
- Bible of Ostervald 1996
- CHENG Yves. Collection practices and exegetical studies of Jesus Christ's words. Entretienschretien.com, [online]. Available on :
  - http://www.entretienschretiens.com/026%20Le%20serpent%20de%20bronze%20-%20Jn%203(14-15).htm
  - http://www.entretienschretiens.com/040%20Loeil%20est%20la%20lampe%20du%20corps%20-%20Mt%206(22-23).htm
  - http://www.entretienschretiens.com/Ta%20foi%20ta%20gueri%20-%20Mc%2010(46-52).htm

- Evaluation of the effectiveness of the practice of hypnosis, 213 p. Edited by INSERM U1178 Mental Health & Public Health: GUEGUEN, BARRY, HASSLER et al. June 2015

- GRONIER Sophie. Hypnoanalgesia in Neurology, 53 p. Memory: THE Medical hypnosis: CHU Felix Guyon (Reunion): 2015. Available at: http://www.hypnose.fr

- KUETU Shora. Bible prophecy: the war between the two posterities. Courcouronnes ANJC Productions, edition 2011, p.168-179. Available on : https://www.tv2vie.org/livres.html

- LAU-TAI-WEN Bertrand. Rapid hypnosis in the operating room, 43 p. Memory: The Medical and Clinical Hypnosis: Reunion: June 2013. Available at: http://www.hypnose.fr

- Unconventional care practices: Complementary Medicine / Alternative / Natural, [online], by the Ministry of Social Affairs and Health in France [ref. of 13.12.16]. Available on : http://social-sante.gouv.fr/soins-et-maladies/qualite-des-soins-et-pratiques/securite/article/pratiques-de-soins-non-conventionnelles

NOTES

Excerpt from an Evaluation Report of the Effectiveness of the Practice of Hypnosis, pp.130-133, 135-137, 143

Review of the scientific literature and literature for professionals

(INSERM [National Institute of the Health and the Medical Research] U1178 Mental Health & Public Health), Juliette Gueguen, Caroline Barry Christine Hassler, Bruno Falissard with the critical expertise of Arnaud Fauconnier and Elisabeth Fournier-Charrière, in June 2015.

SAFETY OF THE HYPNOSIS

[...]

RESULTS

The literature review did not identify clinical case description or prospective study concerned with the safety of the hypnosis. We present only the safety data reported by the trials and magazines presented in the first part concerning the assessment of effectiveness.

COMPARATIVE STUDY

Of the 16 trials identified, 9 were interested in the side effects, whether or not associated with hypnosis.

Only four studies reported the collection of adverse events directly associated with hypnosis (Lindfors, Unge and al.; Moser Tragner and al.; Werner Uldbjerg and al., Elkins, Marcus and al 2008). In these 4 trials, no adverse events attributable to hypnosis were reported.

A study mentions the collection of adverse events, as these are directly attributable to hypnosis (Dickson-Spillmann, Haug and al.). They thus collected so wide side effects not typically associated with cessation (with 11 categories of effects collected systematically). The frequency of such effects (headache, dry mouth, constipation, nausea, strange dreams ...) was low in their 2 treatments groups (hypnosis and relaxation) and no statistically significant difference between groups.

Four other studies mention the collection of adverse events that may occur with the waning of a surgical or radiological interventions (Lang, Benotsch, and al. 2000; Lang, Berbaum and al. 2006; Lang, Berbaum and al. 2008; Marc, Rainville and al. 2008).

- In test (Mark, Rainville and al. 2008), the following adverse events were reported:

During the procedure (5/172 vs 2/175 in the hypnosis group in the control group)

- In the hypnosis group: 1 case of uterine atony, 3 episodes of hemodynamic instability (vagal reactions), 1 episode of vomiting

- In the control group: 1 uterine perforation, 1 episode of hemodynamic instability (vasovagal reaction).

In the recovery room

- In the hypnosis group: 6/172 episodes of nausea / vomiting, dizziness episodes of 5/172 and 10/172 drowsiness

- In the control group: 8/175 episodes of nausea / vomiting, dizziness episodes of 6/175, 7/175 and drowsiness.

- In the study (Lang, Benotsch and al. 2000), the occurrence of hemodynamic instability was more frequent in the standard group than in the hypnosis group (12/79 vs. 1/82). There was no significant difference in the other categories of reported side effects.

- In the trial (Lang, Berbaum and al. 2006), 7 adverse events (bruising, vomiting or vasovagal reaction) have been reported in the standard care group, 11 in the empathy group (hematoma or vagal) and 3 the hypnosis group (hematoma), with no statistically significant difference between groups.

- In the trial (Lang, Berbaum and al. 2008), the frequency of occurrence of adverse events was 12% in the hypnosis group, versus 26% in the standard treatment group and 48% in the empathy group (statistically significant difference). The high prevalence of adverse events in the empathy group resulted in a premature termination of the study.

SYSTEMATIC REVIEWS OF LITERATURE

Data Cochrane reviews are reassuring. However, the total numbers remain low (about 2500 patients). One cannot exclude the existence of serious side effects, but if such effects exist they are of relatively low incidence.

Cochrane Reviews

- The review of Madden (Madden, Middleton and al.) on hypnosis in the management of pain during labour and delivery (total number = 1213) did not find significant difference in occurrence of adverse events (neonatal intensive care, maternal readmissions readmission of new-borns admitted in intensive care mothers) between hypnosis and control groups. Previously, a systematic review of the literature on hypnosis during labour and delivery (Cyna, McAuliffe and al. 2004), cited by the Cochrane review, has not been any side effects from hypnosis.

- The review of Sado (Sado, Ota and al.) on hypnosis to prevent postpartum depression reported no adverse effects.

- The review of Webb (Webb, Kukuruzovic and al. 2007) on the use of hypnotherapy in the management of irritable bowel syndrome (total number = 147) reported no side effects from hypnosis.

- The review (Izquierdo de Santiago and Khan 2007) on the use of hypnotherapy in the treatment of schizophrenia reported no adverse effects.

- The review of Barnes (Barnes, Dong and al.) on the hypnotherapy for smoking cessation (total number = 1120) reported no adverse effects.

- Review of Al-Harasi (Al-Harasi, Ashley and al.) the use of hypnosis in dental care in children (total number = 69) reported no adverse effects attributable to hypnosis.

[...]

In his article *Hypnosis: Critical Issues*, Dr. Daniel Annequin evokes the risk of mental manipulation and recalled that the practice of hypnosis has been repeatedly complained in Britain and the United States in the production of false memories of trauma and sexual abuse in childhood. He believes that *"the limit these risks through better selection of therapists with precise specifications regarding the content of the training and monitoring of graduates."*

Ernst, in his critical guide on the alternative medicine (Ernst 2005) recalls that the information obtained under hypnosis are likely to fall under fabrication. Moreover, is mentioned that in hypnosis, "the recall to consciousness of repressed memories can be painful," which can potentially exacerbate underlying problems.

More generally, the question of the ethical-legal risk and risk of psychological manipulation is addressed by practitioners in hypnosis, as evidenced by a recent report on the subject (Keke 2014).

To date, in the absence of clear legal framework, codes of ethics are often offered by the associations of practitioners for example, the CFHTB [Francophone Confederation of Hypnosis and Brief Therapies].

[...]

JURISPRUDENCE

- On the site of the jurisprudence of [National Council of the College of medical doctors in France], there is no reported case law condemning the practice of hypnosis by a doctor. A case mentioning hypnosis is referenced but it is a condemnation of a doctor for advertising on his internet activity (File cdn9819).

- A medical hypnosis of University Degree is being interested in **the ethical-legal risk in hypnosis** identified 16 judgments involving hypnosis, including 15 concerning events that took place in France (Keke 2014). These were mostly cases of rape or sexual abuse of patients / persons placed under hypnosis by their practitioner / one third of cases of illegal practice of medicine, or the use of hypnosis for the procedures of justice.

The sexual assaults cases (n = 6) incriminate 1 doctor in 2 cases, 1 osteopath in 1 case, 1 "hypnotist" in 1 case, 1 "hypnotist" no doctor in 1 case, and someone close (friend / family) in the last case.

STATEMENTS OF LOSS

The Legal documentation Information Service of MACSF [Mutual insurance Company of the French healthcare] informed us that no loss in connection with this practice had not been declared (personal communication, July 2014).
- Furthermore, given the ethical and legal issues, a reflection of management (including and especially legislative) of the practice of hypnosis seems also relevant.

SUMMARY OF RESULTS

In total, the data on safety of the hypnosis are reassuring. There were no reports of serious adverse events attributable to hypnosis. However, one cannot exclude their existence, but if such effects exist their impact is relatively small.

The challenge seems rather to be at the ethical and legal level. Already, the practice of the hypnosis is framed by ethical charters, but there are not so far from clear legal framework to better define the risk. It appears, however, very limited when hypnosis is used as a complementary tool by healthcare professionals already trained and qualified otherwise.
Similarly, there is then no risk of delay or hindrance to conventional management would be required. This is often the case for hypnosis since the ethics charter CFHTB sets using hypnosis as a complementary tool. **Hypnosis is one of the most integrated unconventional practices to conventional care offer**, which limits the risks associated with an "alternative" remedies. Nevertheless, in France, hypnosis is not only offered by way of integrative healthcare professionals. It can be offered by non-medical professionals, and we cannot exclude that it can be offered alternatively. It is therefore important to remember the risk inherent in any alternative use unconventional therapies: to delay one or hinder access to conventional cares that would otherwise be necessary.
[...]
Regarding the safety of the practice of the hypnosis:
- As further practice, a reflection on the establishment of **surveillance system** (equivalent to pharmacovigilance) seems relevant, in order to collect data from the field and provide a better understanding of the potential side effects associated with the practice.

- Furthermore, since the ethical and legal issues, a reflection of management (including and especially legislative) of the practice of hypnosis seems also relevant.

ISBN 978-2-9561617-3-8
Legal deposit on August 2017

Printed in the United States of America
By Lulu.com

www.ingramcontent.com/pod-product-compliance
Ingram Content Group UK Ltd.
Pitfield, Milton Keynes, MK11 3LW, UK
UKHW021127260726
13994UKWH00001B/16